Personal, Social and Health Educ

TIME TO TALK

BOOK 1
for ages 4/5

Jim Green

CollinsEducational

Published by Collins Educational
An imprint of HarperCollins*Publishers* Ltd
77-85 Fulham Palace Road
London W6 8JB

Reprinted 1995, 1996 (twice)

ISBN 0 00 318790 X

Commissioning editor
Graham Bradbury

Edited by
Paula Hammond

Production by
Angela Davies

Design and page layout by
Carla Turchini

Illustrated by
Helen Herbert
Maureen Carter

Printed and bound in the UK by Redwood Books, Trowbridge, Wiltshire.

Contents

Contents of the three **Time to Talk** books

Book 

Book 2

I am growing
GROWING AND CHANGING

I can play
CO-OPERATION

When I started school
SHARING MEMORIES

Let me tell you
COMMUNICATION

Eating and drinking
IMPORTANCE OF FOOD

Happy and sad
HANDLING EMOTIONS

Invitations
TIMES OF CELEBRATION

Family outings
COMMUNICATION SKILLS

Helping and hurting
PERSONAL RELATIONSHIPS

When I am ill
CARE IN ILLNESS

Good and bad
MAKING JUDGEMENTS

Come and visit
ORGANIZATION SKILLS

The clinic
LOCAL HEALTH CARE ENVIRONMENT

My school
THE SCHOOL ENVIRONMENT

Places I like to visit
THE WIDER ENVIRONMENT

People I see
PEOPLE IN THE COMMUNITY

Busy places
SERVICES IN THE COMMUNITY

Quiet places
THE SOUND ENVIRONMENT

Book 3

Yes and no
RESPONSIBLE CHOICES

Right and wrong
MORAL JUDGEMENTS

When I started school
CHANGING AND GROWING

Look what I can do
DEVELOPING SKILLS

When you are as old as me
AGEING

I am changing
THE MATURING PROCESS

I know who I am
FAMILY MEMBERSHIP

Goodbye
COPING WITH LOSS

Let's celebrate
TIMES OF CELEBRATION

Who looks after me?
CARERS

Happy and sad
FRIENDSHIP

Telling the truth
HONESTY

Things that belong to us all
THE COMMUNITY ENVIRONMENT

Am I safe?
PERSONAL SAFETY

Getting around
TRANSPORT AND MOBILITY

What I do after school
HOME PASTIMES

Where I live
UNDERSTANDING THE LOCAL ENVIRONMENT

I wish we had
LOCAL AMENITIES

Time to Talk

INTRODUCTION

This book is made up of three themes: **Myself**, **My Family and Friends** and **Where I Live**. These themes are designed to help you to promote personal and social awareness in children – to help them develop a sense of their own identity and place it in the context of who they meet and where they live.

The material in this book provides learning activities which place before children, in an appropriate way, some of the issues which are central to healthy growth and development. By using *Time to Talk* it is hoped that the children will be encouraged to become aware of their own and others' physical identity and will grow in an understanding of their own uniqueness and the uniqueness of others. This building of a sense of self-identity will be complemented by exploring how we share so much with others and they with us, thus forming the basis of a sense of community.

Each of the three themes contains six 'lessons' which deal with a specific area of Personal, Social and Health Education. The time needed for each 'lesson' will vary according to individual needs and circumstances.

MANAGEMENT NOTES

Each lesson contains a full page of management notes, which are meant as guidelines on how the lesson might be developed. Within the management notes teachers will find guidance on:

Preparation

Preparation sets out details of what needs to be done, in advance, to prepare for the lesson.

Discussion

In each case the *Discussion* notes give examples of points worth bringing out during the discussion, as well as suggested possible strategies to use – questions to raise with the children, or ideas for activities that tie-in with the topic of discussion. However, the suggested questions are only meant to illustrate one of the ways discussion of the topic might go. Discussion is best directed and controlled but should never be made rigid and inflexible, as talk is often a time for expression, exploration and learning from one another.

It is assumed that in this area of the curriculum, particularly, discussion is vital. The children should, therefore, gather for discussion in a way that is

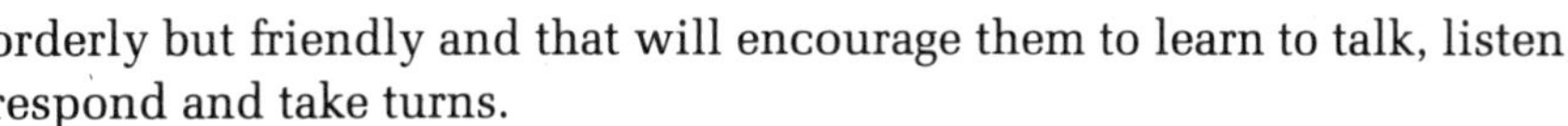

orderly but friendly and that will encourage them to learn to talk, listen, respond and take turns.

Follow-up activity

The notes on the *Follow-up activity* are meant to explain and expand on work on the 'activity copymaster' (see below).

COPYMASTERS

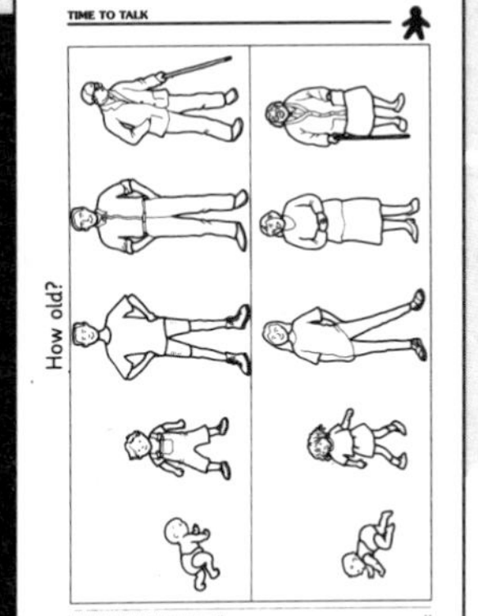

Each lesson also includes three photocopiable 'copymasters':

Follow-up activity copymaster

The first copymaster provides a practical activity which will reinforce and develop the theme of the particular lesson. A *Follow-up activity copymaster* is therefore provided for each lesson, although there could be many activities to follow up discussions, and the one provided can be replaced with something more appropriate if you so wish.

Song/poem/story/game copymaster

Children love songs, poems, stories and games – and one of these is provided for each lesson. These sheets are designed to be photocopied and can be used in a variety of ways – for example, they can be coloured in by the children, used in class, taken home, or enlarged as part of a classroom display.

Where songs are provided they can be sung to the well-known tunes suggested or chanted to a steady rhythm. They need no special musical skills. Sometimes the songs and poems encourage actions to be used with the words. These actions are generally illustrated on the copymaster so that, even if children can not read the words they and others (should they take the sheets home) can see what they are required to do.

In general the song, poem, story or game copymaster will be self explanatory. Occasionally, however, extra guidance or ideas to expand on the copymaster will be given in the management notes.

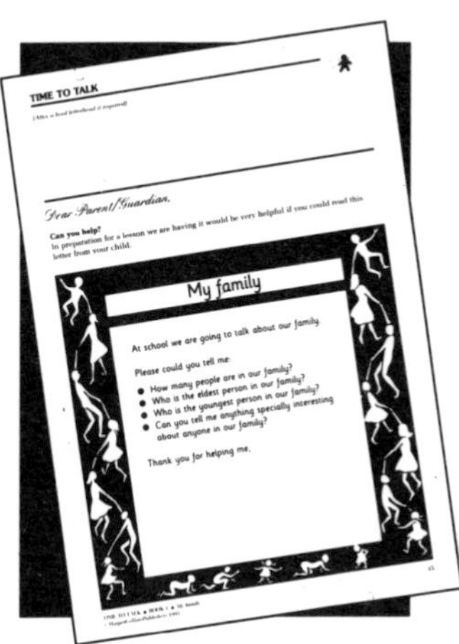

Can you help? copymaster

The *Can you help? copymasters* are for use in a one-to-one situation, if this can be arranged. Personal and social development must seek to be centred on the individual. Children desperately need to talk and be listened to as individuals. However, it is not always practical or desirable for the teacher to do all the talking and listening. These copymasters are designed, therefore, to be used both in and out of school. Sometimes they will be best used at home, sometimes in school with the teacher or another adult. They can form a vital link with parents. However, the situation of each school and each household is so different that the copymasters are designed to be suitably varied and flexible, for as many situations as possible.

It is hoped that *Time to Talk* will support teachers in placing before children rich and appropriate learning activities. It is a resource to develop, change, adapt and build on. In using *Time to Talk* we hope you will see children grow and develop, both as healthy individuals, and as members of their communities.

1

I am special

SIGNIFICANCE OF NAMES

Aims

- to help children realize that their names are important and have meaning.
- to make it clear where names come from and what purpose they serve.

Preparation

Before the lesson, send home photocopies of the **Can you help? copymaster** for discussion between the child and parent/guardian.

Make a large name flash card for each of the children.

Make enough copies of the **Make a name badge copymaster** so that all the children can have one each, and write in each child's name.

Make photocopies of the **We are very special song**, as necessary.

TIME TO TALK

We are very special

(A song sung to the tune of "Here We Go Round The Mulberry Bush".)

We are the children in this class
in this class
in this class
We are the children in this class
And we are very special.

We are the boys and we are the girls
we are the girls
we are the girls
We are the boys and we are the girls
And we are very special.

We can work and we can play
we can play
we can play
We can work and we can play
So we are very special.

Can you think of actions to go with this poem?

Discussion

Points to bring out

- Family names are received.
- 'Special' names (forenames) are chosen for the child and are, therefore, unique to every child.

Strategies to try

What names do we have in the class?

Which is our family name and which is/are our own special name(s)?

Who chose our name(s) for us?

Were we given our name on a special occasion?

What do we know about our name?

Do we all have different special names?

Do we all have different family names?

Can we recognize our own names?

Can we recognize other people's names? *(Show the flash cards to see if the children can recognize them.)*

Follow-up activity

Put the children into groups and give each group its set of name badges. Ask the children:

Can you find your own name? Help each other.

The children can decorate and cut out their badges and then use sellotape to stick them on and wear them.

Make a name badge

We are very special

(A song sung to the tune of "Here We Go Round The Mulberry Bush".)

We are the children in this class
in this class
in this class
We are the children in this class

And we are very special.

We are the boys and we are the girls
we are the girls
we are the girls
We are the boys and we are the girls

And we are very special.

We can work and we can play
we can play
we can play
We can work and we can play

Can you think of actions to go with this poem?

So we are very special.

[Affix school letterhead if required]

Dear Parent/Guardian,

Can you help?
In preparation for a lesson we are having it would be very helpful if you could read this letter from your child.

I am special

At school we are going to talk about our names as part of our lesson called "I am special".

Please could you tell me:

- How many names do I have?
- Were any of these names chosen specially for me?
- Why were those names chosen?
- Were they given to me on a special occasion?
- Do the names I was given mean anything special?

Thank you for helping me,

Myself

2

I am young, you are old

UNDERSTANDING AGEING

Aims

- ▶ to raise awareness of the fact that, as time passes, we all grow old.
- ▶ to get the children to understand how old age comes about.
- ▶ to make children aware that old people are real people with real lives.

Preparation

Before the lesson, arrange for each child to use a photocopy of the **Can you help? copymaster** with an adult. If the children decide to ask a member of their family to help, try to encourage some of them to ask grandmas and granddads as well as mums and dads. If children are working with adults in school, try to make the age span as wide as possible.

Make copies of the **How old? copymaster** and **The difference game**, as necessary.

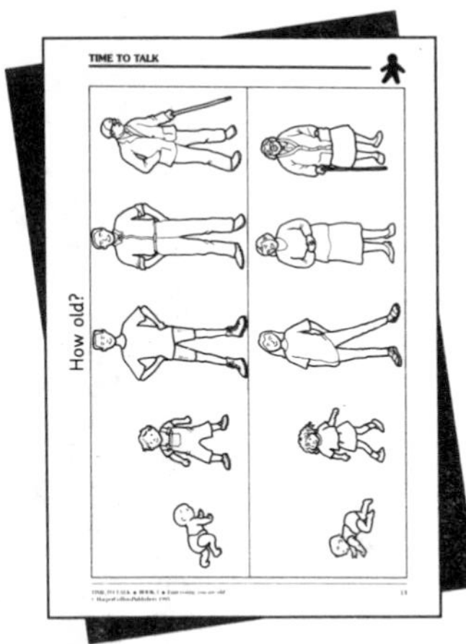

Discussion

Points to bring out

- We are young now, but we will all get older.
- Ageing is a natural process, and is nothing to be afraid of.

Strategies to try

Do we all know how old we are?

Are we young or are we old?

Do any of you know any old people? *(Let's make a list of old people that we know.)*

Are old people different from young people? How?

Were old people ever young once?

How did they get old?

Follow-up activity

Give each child a copy of the **How old? copymaster** and ask them to colour in the image most like themselves, the one most like the friend who helped them with the **Can you help? copymaster**, and one other person of their choice.

Game

Choose two children to stand up in front of the class. The class sing the song from **The difference game** copymaster. The first child to say how they are different from the other sits down. Another two children then take their place, and the game and song are repeated.

By carefully choosing the children, a progression of difficulty can be built into the activity (e.g. first pair of children: boy and girl, second pair: girl with long hair and girl with short hair, etc).

How old?

The difference game

(A singing game sung to the tune of "This Old Man".)

All sing:

Look at me, look at me,
Look and see what you can see.
You and I are not the same,
Shall we play the difference game?

[Affix school letterhead if required]

Dear Friend,

Can you help?
In preparation for a lesson we are having it would be very helpful if you could read this letter from one of your children.

I am young, you are old

At school we are going to have a lesson called "I am young, you are old".

Please could you answer these questions to help us in our lesson:

- Do you think you are old?
- How did you stop being young?
- Is being old different from being young?
- Do you like being older than me?
- When you are old do you miss anything?
- When you were about my age were things like they are now?
- Who looked after you when you were young?

Thank you for helping me,

3

I look after myself

LEARNING INDEPENDENCE

Aims

- ▶ to help children to become aware that, as they get older, they grow and change.
- ▶ to discuss how, as they grow, they learn to become more independent and to take more responsibility for looking after themselves.

Preparation

Before the lesson, send home photocopies of the **Can you help? copymaster** for discussion between child and parent/guardian.

TIME TO TALK

Dear Parent/Guardian,

Can you help?
In preparation for a lesson we are having it would be very helpful if you could read this letter from your child.

I look after myself

At school we are goung to have a lesson called "I look after myself".

Please could you tell me

- What could I do when I was born?
- Who looked after me all the time?
- What things do you need to do to look after a baby?
- How old was I before I could dress myself?
- How old was I before I could feed myself?
- Have we any pictures of the clothes I used to wear when I was little?
- Is it hard to look after someone?

Thank you for helping me.

Photocopy a boy or a girl for each child from the **Dressing-up dolls copymaster**.

Make enough copies of the **What do they wear? copymaster** so that all the children can have one each.

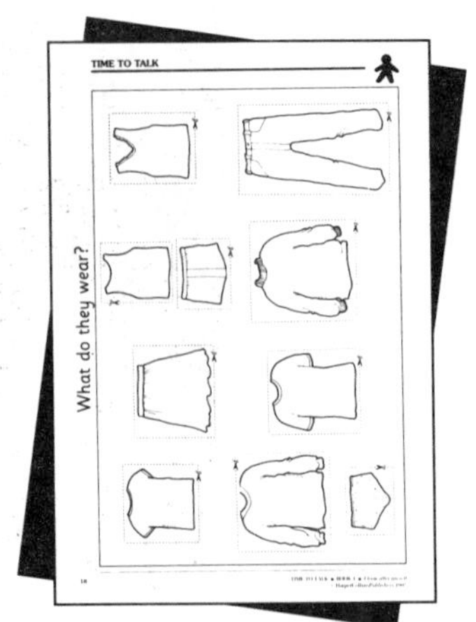

Discussion

Points to bring out

- The children have changed since they were very small.
- They will continue to grow and change all their lives.

Strategies to try

It is important to help the children become aware that there are some things that they can all do (e.g. go to the toilet, get washed) but that there are still some things that none or few of them can (or are allowed) to do, such as cooking or washing-up. The discussion could be developed further to show the differences in the amount of independence each child has.

What things do we do when we get up in the morning? *(Let's make a list.)*

What things on the list do you get help with?

Which things do you do all by yourself?

When you get dressed who chooses your clothes for the day?

Which clothes are easy to put on and which are hard?

Do we have to get dressed and undressed at school? Why?

Did you always dress yourself? Can any of you remember having help washing or going to the toilet?

Can you look after yourself more now than when you were little?

What does it feel like being able to do things for yourself?

Follow-up activity

Give each child a copy of the **Dressing-up dolls copymaster** and the **What do they wear? copymaster**. Each child should have one dressing-up doll each. Decide whether you are going to give the children only pictures of 'dolls' of their own sex or whether you are going to hand out a mix of 'dolls' regardless of the child's sex. Ask the children to cut out the clothes and stick them onto the doll. The children will learn from this activity that external things such as clothes are often interchangeable between the sexes. It is what is *beneath* the clothes that determines whether you are a boy or girl.

Dressing-up dolls

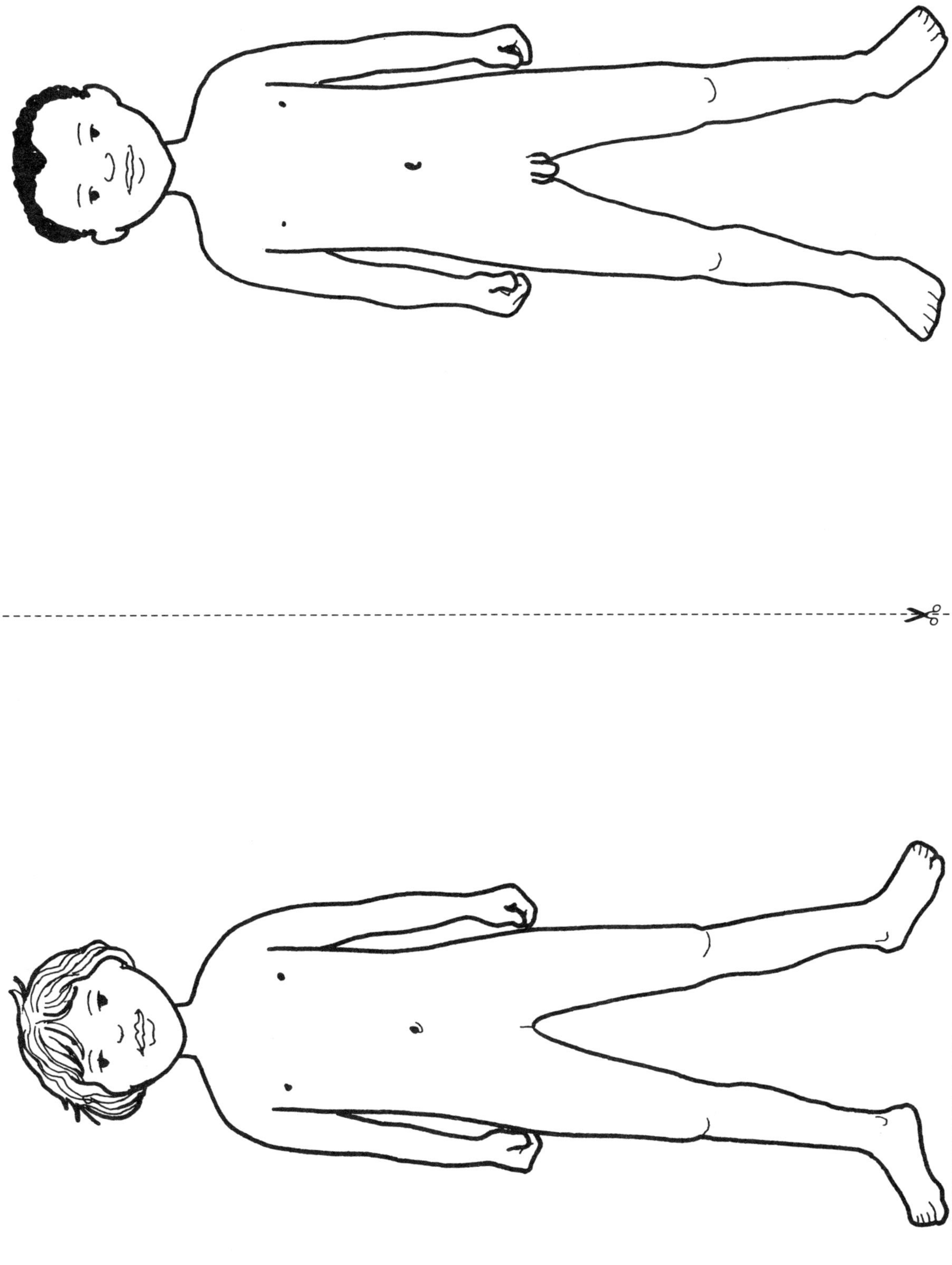

What do they wear?

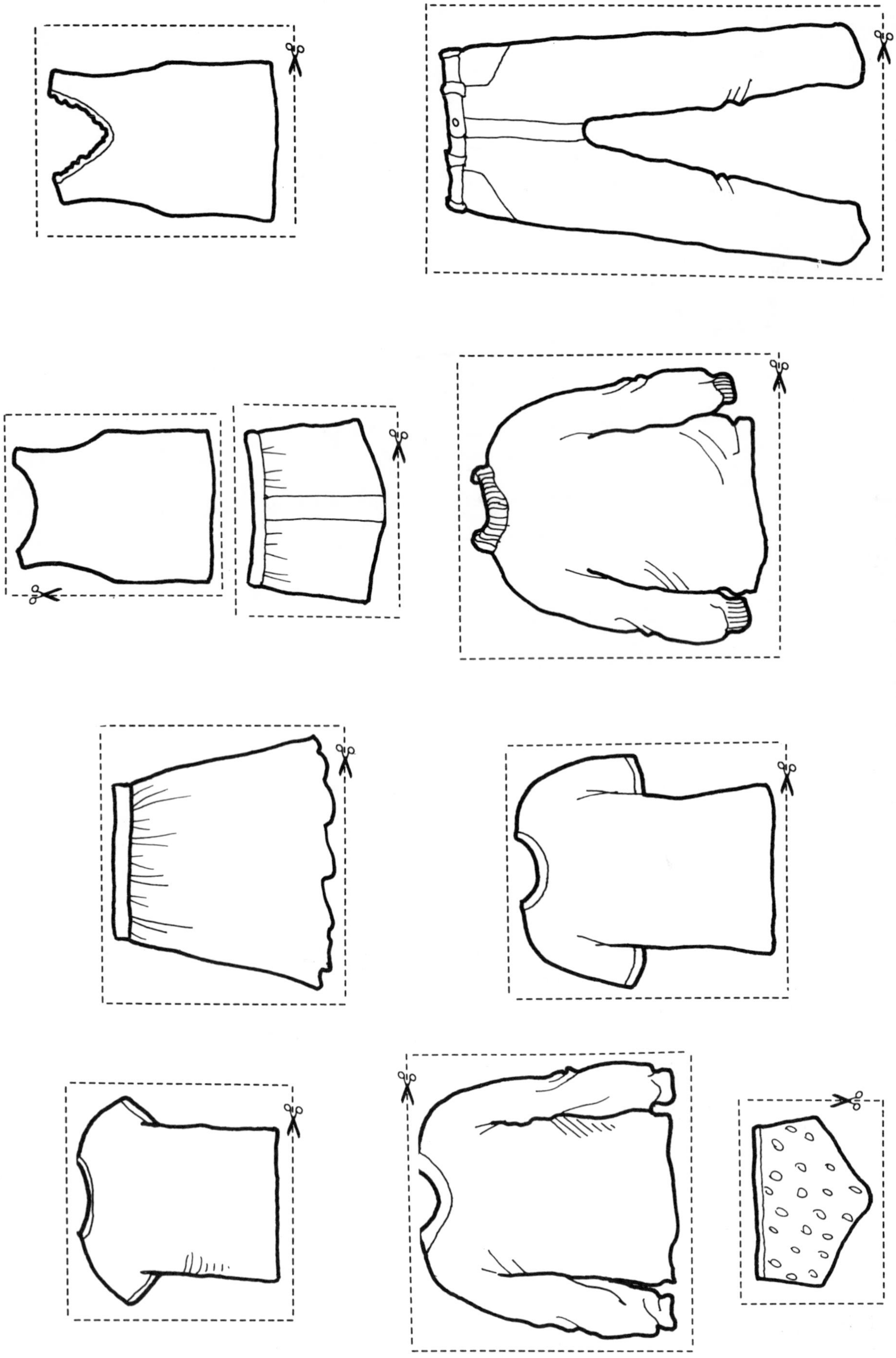

[Affix school letterhead if required]

Dear Parent/Guardian,

Can you help?
In preparation for a lesson we are having it would be very helpful if you could read this letter from your child.

I look after myself

At school we are goung to have a lesson called "I look after myself".

Please could you tell me:

- What could I do when I was born?
- Who looked after me all the time?
- What things do you need to do to look after a baby?
- How old was I before I could dress myself?
- How old was I before I could feed myself?
- Have we any pictures of the clothes I used to wear when I was little?
- Is it hard to look after someone?

Thank you for helping me,

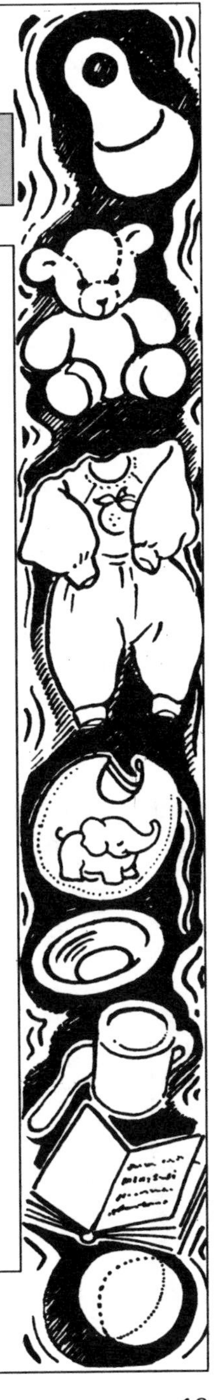

4 Things I like

APPRECIATING
OUR ENVIRONMENT

Aims

- to make a songbook about 'things we like'.
- to get the children to think about the rich variety of things that are available for us to enjoy.

Preparation

Before the lesson, send home photocopies of the **Can you help? copymaster** for discussion between the child and parent/guardian.

TIME TO TALK

Dear Parent/Guardian,

Can you help?
In preparation for a lesson we are having it would be very helpful if you could read this letter from your child.

Things I like

At school we are going to talk about our favourite things. Please will you look at these four pictures and tell me which one you like best and why?

Spring | Summer | Autumn | Winter

Thank you for helping me.

Make enough copies of the **My favourite thing copymaster** so that all of the children can have a sheet each.

Make photocopies of the **I like... song** as necessary.

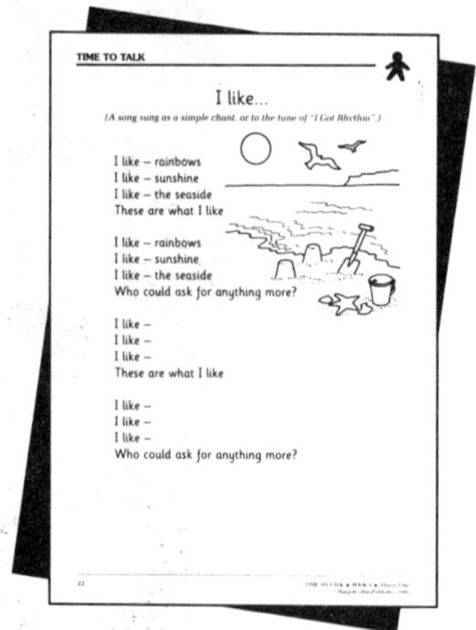

TIME TO TALK

I like...

(A song sung as a simple chant, or to the tune of "I Got Rhythm".)

I like – rainbows
I like – sunshine
I like – the seaside
These are what I like

I like – rainbows
I like – sunshine
I like – the seaside
Who could ask for anything more?

I like –
I like –
I like –
These are what I like

I like –
I like –
I like –
Who could ask for anything more?

Discussion

Points to bring out

- There are many things, bought, made, free and natural for us to enjoy.

Strategies to try

Tell the children that, as a class, they are going to make a songbook about the things they like. Ask them to think about all the things that are available for us to enjoy.

Are there many different things we like?
Are the things we like all expensive?
Where do they come from?
Are there some things we all like?
Are there some things we like that others don't?
What is your favourite thing?

During the discussion make a note of all the 'favourite things' that the children mention. This list can be used to help the children with ideas during the follow-up activity, if necessary.

Follow-up activity

Give each child a copy of the **My favourite thing copymaster** and ask them to draw and colour a favourite thing on the page.
(If any children have problems deciding what it is that they like, use the list made during the discussion to refresh their memories.) Collect in the pictures and bind them together to form a songbook.

Song

The songbook can be used to help the children sing the **I like... song**. In each case allow the children to start a line, while you end it with an object from one of the pictures collected in the songbook. If the song is to sound 'right' some care must be taken about how many beats the word or phrase uses. However if short single words or longer phrases are mixed the song can become more fun to sing. If you choose to hand out copies of the song, help the children to complete the two unfinished verses and get them to draw pictures to go with them.

My favourite thing

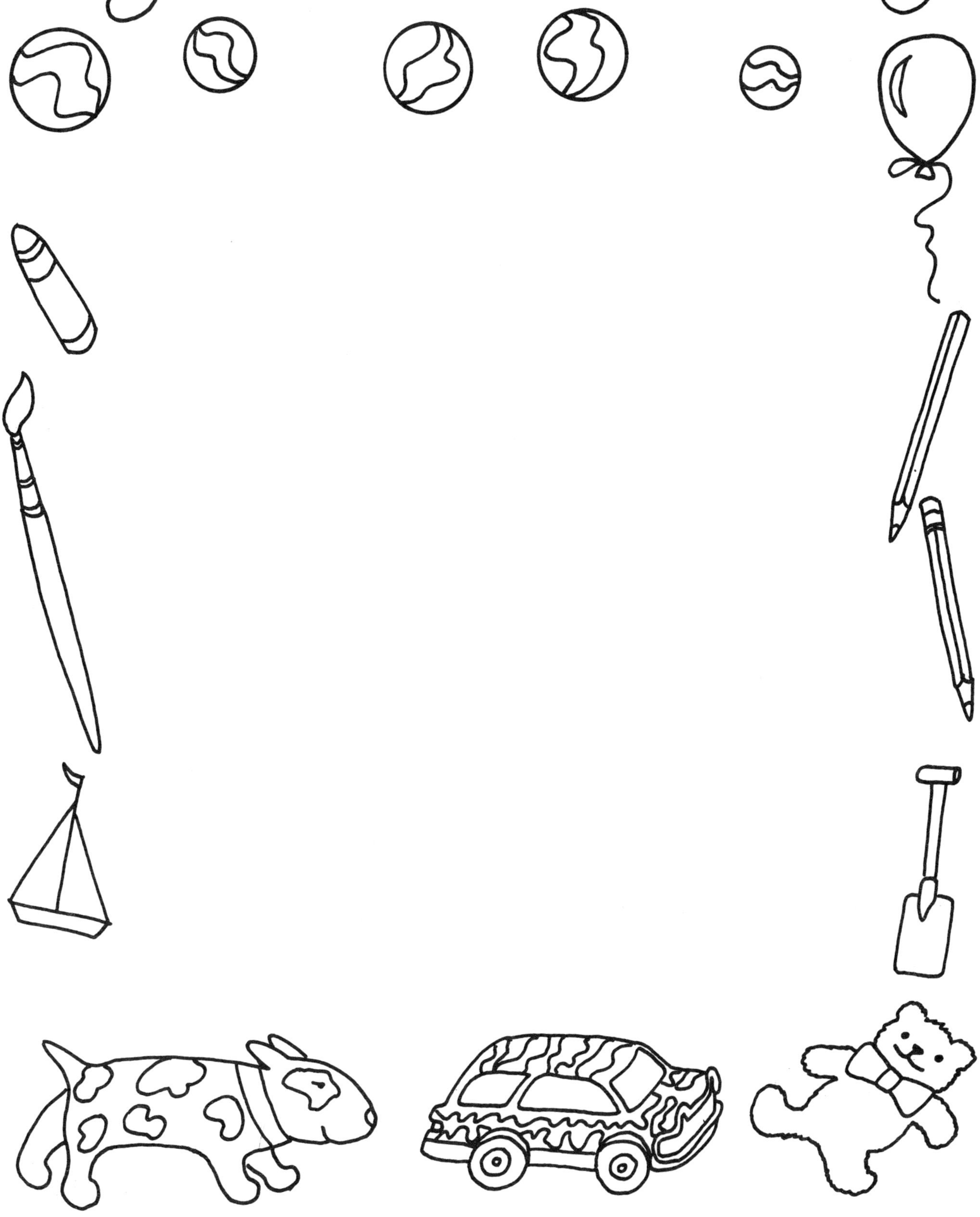

I like...

(A song sung as a simple chant, or to the tune of "I Got Rhythm".)

I like – rainbows
I like – sunshine
I like – the seaside
These are what I like

I like – rainbows
I like – sunshine
I like – the seaside
Who could ask for anything more?

I like –
I like –
I like –
These are what I like

I like –
I like –
I like –
Who could ask for anything more?

[Affix school letterhead if required]

Dear Parent/Guardian,

Can you help?
In preparation for a lesson we are having it would be very helpful if you could read this letter from your child.

Things I like

At school we are going to talk about our favourite things. Please will you look at these four pictures and tell me which one you like best and why?

Thank you for helping me,

5

Things I can do

PERSONAL HYGIENE

Aims

- to raise awareness of the fact that there are some things that we can all do, and that there are some things that only some of us can do.
- to lead children on to consider how they keep themselves clean.

Preparation

Find an older person who can come into the classroom and talk about 'something I can do'. This could be someone who knits, gardens, paints, crochets, plays a sport, cooks or collects. The important thing is that the person can talk to, and listen to, very young children. Ask the visitor to go through the **Can you help? copymaster** with the whole class and answer the questions it asks. This talk should take place about a day or two before the class discussion.

Make enough copies of the **Keeping clean copymaster** and the **I can... poem** so that all the children can have one each.

TIME TO TALK

Keeping clean

Colour in the things we need to keep ourselves clean.

Discussion

Points to bring out

- Hobbies and pastimes are fun, but sometimes take time to learn or develop.
- There are ordinary things that we all do.
- Keeping clean is an ordinary thing, but it is still very important.

Strategies to try

Do you remember our visitor who came to talk to us about —-?

Some of the things we do are special things called hobbies or pastimes.

A lot of the things we do are ordinary – things that we all do.

Here are some ordinary things: eating, playing, sleeping, talking.

Can you think of any ordinary things everyone does? *If washing is mentioned, stop there. If washing isn't mentioned then mime washing your hands and face and ask:*

Who can wash themselves?

Why do we wash ourselves?

What would happen if we didn't wash?

When do we wash? Do you know why we wash at these times?
(We should especially wash our hands after going to the toilet and before eating.)

Follow-up activity

Give each child a copy of the **Keeping clean copymaster** and ask them to colour in **only** the items that they need to keep themselves clean and tidy.

Poem

Teach the children the **I can... poem**. Encourage them to make up actions to go with the poem and, if there is time, work together to produce another verse which emphasises the importance of personal hygiene.

Keeping clean

Colour in the things we need to keep ourselves clean.

I can...

I can stand
I can shout
I can jump
And run about

I can smile
I can cry
I can watch
The birds that fly

I can dress
I can eat
I can wash
My face and feet!

I can sleep
I can wake
I can eat
A piece of cake

I can hear
I can see
I can tell you
I am me!

Can you think of actions to go with this poem?

[Affix school letterhead if required]

Dear Friend,

Can you help?
The children would like to invite you to take part in a lesson. In preparation it would be very helpful if you could read this letter from our class.

Things I can do

At school we are going to talk about the different things that we can do. Would you come and talk to us about something special you can do?

Please could you tell me:

- Could you always do this?
- How and when did you start?
- Did someone help you?
- Did you have to practise?
- Do you enjoy it? Why?
- Is it nice to have something you can do well?
- Do you share what you can do with others?

Thank you for helping us,

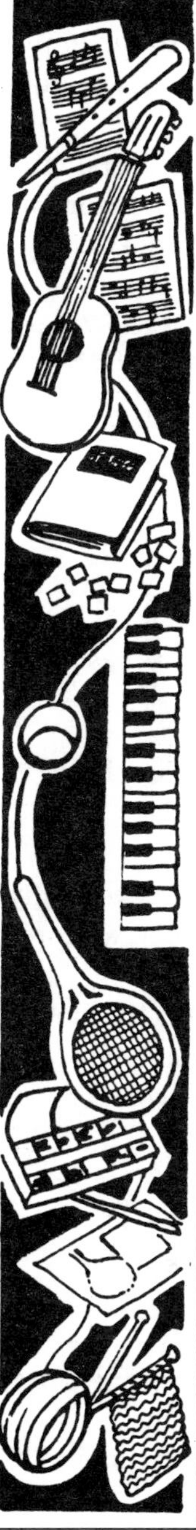

6
Feelings

HANDLING EMOTIONS

Aims

- to raise awareness of the fact that we all have different feelings at different times.
- to get children to realize that our feelings affect the way we behave.
- to make children aware that some feelings are good and that some feelings are bad.

Preparation

Before the lesson, send home photocopies of the **Can you help? copymaster** for discussion between child and parent/guardian.

Make enough photocopies of the **I made teddy copymaster** so that all the children can have one each.

TIME TO TALK

Tilly's Special Day

When Tilly woke one Saturday morning it was especially early because it was a very special day. She jumped out of bed and ran downstairs. In the kitchen her dad was reading a newspaper and drinking tea. "Good morning, Tilly", he said. "You're up early."

Tilly looked at her dad to see if he knew it was a very special day, but he went on reading his paper and drinking his tea. "Has the postman been?" asked Tilly. She thought that, as it was a very special day, there might be something special for her in the post. "Yes", replied her dad. "The letters are there by the clock."

Tilly looked at the letters. Two brown envelopes and a brightly coloured one. "What are they?" she asked. "Bills and a free offer", replied her dad. "There's never anything interesting in the post these days." "Anything special?" asked Tilly. Her dad shook his head. Tilly sat at the table. The day didn't look like it was going to be special so far. No one was taking any notice of her and there was nothing special for her in the post. No one seemed to care about her special day. Perhaps, she thought sadly, it won't be a special day after all. Perhaps it will just be an ordinary day like any other day.

Sadly, Tilly got up from the table and went to the front room to watch TV. She opened the door and hanging on the wall, in bright shiny red letters, was HAPPY BIRTHDAY TILLY. Her mum stood by a table where there was a pile of envelopes all addressed to Tilly. There were boxes of presents, some in coloured wrapping and some in brown paper with stamps on. Dad came in carrying a tray with cereal and juice, and on a plate was a slice of toast with one lighted candle in it! Mum and dad sang "Happy birthday to Tilly" and then she blew the candle out. "That's just to start your special day, Tilly", said Mum. "At tea we'll have your real cake with all the candles and a party." Tilly felt really happy because it was a very special day after all.

Copy the **Tilly's special day story**, as appropriate.

Ask all the children to bring in a stamped, self-addressed envelope.

Discussion

Points to bring out

- That events affect our feelings – when bad things happen it makes us feel sad, when good things happen it makes us feel happy.

Strategies to try

Read the **Tilly's special day story**. At appropriate places in the story ask the children:

Have you ever felt excited?
What makes people feel excited?
Have you ever felt sad?
What makes people feel sad?
Have you ever felt happy?
What makes people feel happy?
Which is nicer, happy or sad? Why?
Is it nice to make someone feel sad?
Is it nice to make someone feel happy?

Follow-up activity

Are people happy when they get nice things in the post?

Give out the **I made teddy copymaster**. Tell the children to choose a happy/sad/excited/tired head for their teddy, and cut it out and stick it on to the teddy's body. If they are able, ask them to fill in the statement "I made teddy —— (happy, sad, etc) for you". When they have finished get them to put their teddy in the envelope. The envelopes can be addressed to their parents/guardians at their home address so that the postman will deliver the teddy and make it a special day.

I made teddy

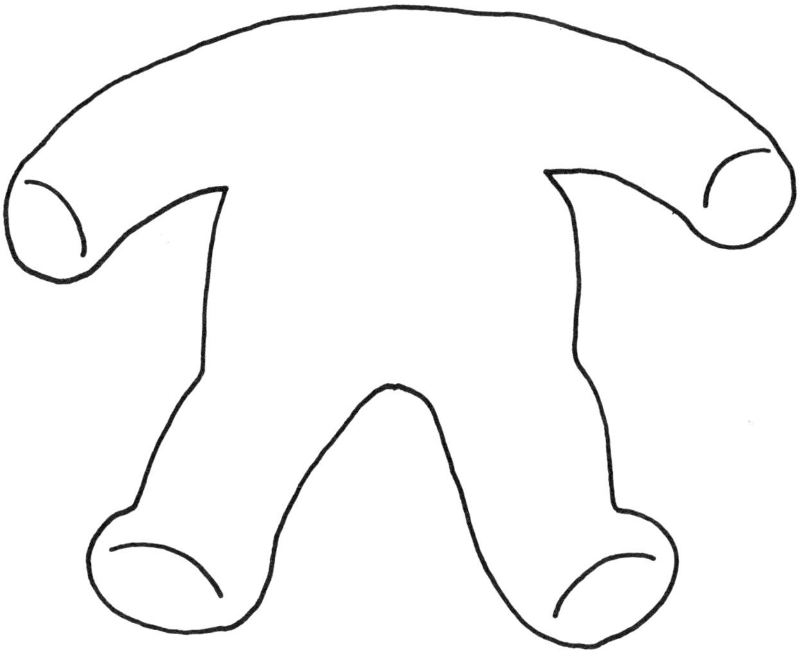

I made teddy ________________ for you.

happy sad excited tired

Tilly's Special Day

When Tilly woke one Saturday morning it was especially early because it was a very special day. She jumped out of bed and ran downstairs. In the kitchen her dad was reading a newspaper and drinking tea. "Good morning, Tilly", he said. "You're up early."

Tilly looked at her dad to see if he knew it was a very special day, but he went on reading his paper and drinking his tea. "Has the postman been?" asked Tilly. She thought that, as it was a very special day, there might be something special for her in the post. "Yes", replied her dad. "The letters are there by the clock."

Tilly looked at the letters. Two brown envelopes and a brightly coloured one. "What are they?" she asked. "Bills and a free offer", replied her dad. "There's never anything interesting in the post these days." "Anything special?" asked Tilly. Her dad shook his head. Tilly sat at the table. The day didn't look like it was going to be special so far. No one was taking any notice of her and there was nothing special for her in the post. No one seemed to care about her special day. Perhaps, she thought sadly, it won't be a special day after all. Perhaps it will just be an ordinary day like any other day.

Sadly, Tilly got up from the table and went to the front room to watch TV. She opened the door and hanging on the wall, in bright shiny red letters, was HAPPY BIRTHDAY TILLY. Her mum stood by a table where there was a pile of envelopes all addressed to Tilly. There were boxes of presents, some in coloured wrapping and some in brown paper with stamps on. Dad came in carrying a tray with cereal and juice, and on a plate was a slice of toast with one lighted candle in it! Mum and dad sang "Happy birthday to Tilly" and then she blew the candle out. "That's just to start your special day, Tilly", said Mum. "At tea we'll have your real cake with all the candles and a party." Tilly felt really happy because it was a very special day after all.

[Affix school letterhead if required]

Dear Parent/Guardian,

Can you help?
In preparation for a lesson we are having it would be very helpful if you could read this letter from your child.

Feelings

At school we are going to talk about things that make us happy and things that make us sad, as part of our lesson called “Feelings”.

Everybody is happy sometimes.

- Can you tell me a story about yourself which is a happy story?

Everybody is sad sometimes.

- Can you tell me a story about yourself which is a sad story?

Thank you for helping me,

FAMILY MEMBERSHIP

7

My family

Aim

▶ to help the children to understand that all families are different.

Preparation

Before the lesson, send home photocopies of the **Can you help? copymaster** for discussion between child and parent/guardian.

TIME TO TALK

Dear Parent/Guardian,

Can you help?
In preparation for a lesson we are having it would be very helpful if you could read this letter from your child.

My family

At school we are going to talk about our family.

Please could you tell me:

- How many people are in our family?
- Who is the eldest person in our family?
- Who is the youngest person in our family?
- Can you tell me anything specially interesting about anyone in our family?

Thank you for helping me,

Make enough copies of the **My family copymaster** so that all the children can have at least one each. (Some children, with particularly large families, may need more than one sheet.)

Make photocopies of the **Teddy gets a family story**, as necessary.

TIME TO TALK

Teddy gets a family

"Does everyone have a family?" asked Tom as his mum tucked him into bed. "I suppose so", said his mum.

"Everyone in the whole world?" asked Tom. "Well," said Mum, "some people might not have a family."

"Why not?" asked Tom.

"Well, their family might have died or got lost in a war or a disaster."

Tom thought for a moment. "And would they be sad?"

"Yes", said Mum. "It must be very sad to lose your family, but don't worry, you won't lose us."

"Not ever?" said Tom.

"Well, perhaps when you are grown up", replied Mum.

"I know someone who hasn't got a family", said Tom suddenly.

"Oh dear", said Mum. "That's very sad. Who is it?"

"It's Teddy", replied Tom. "He hasn't got a family."

"Aren't we Teddy's family?" asked Mum.

"We are in a way," said Tom, "but we're not his real family. Tomorrow I'll give Teddy a family of his own."

"What a good idea", said Mum, smiling. "I have an old Teddy of mine who can be his grandma."

Tom smiled a tired smile. He was so happy because tomorrow Teddy would have a real family of his own.

Discussion

Points to bring out

- Families can be large or small.
- Some families all live together in the same house.
- Some families live in different parts of the country/world.

Strategies to try

Does your family all live together in the same place?
Do you have family members in different parts of the country/world?
Who thinks they have the biggest family?
Who thinks they have the smallest family?
Who has the oldest person in a family?
Who has the youngest person in a family?
Who can tell me anything interesting about someone in their family?

During the discussion it may emerge that the children all have different impressions of what exactly a family is. Some children will talk exclusively about the people that they actually live with as their family. Other children will include relatives that live outside of the family home.

Follow-up activity

Get the children to cut out the appropriate figures from the **My family copymaster**, stick them on to a sheet of paper and colour them in to create a picture of their 'family'. They will need to think about how many people there are in their family so as to be able to choose a suitable size of paper.

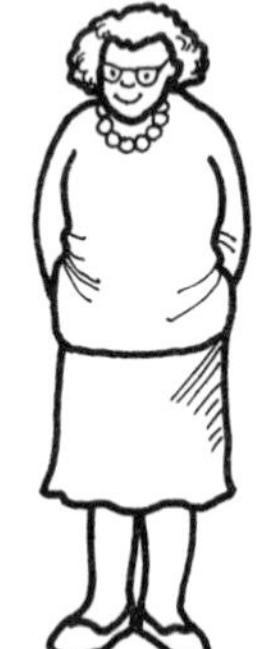

My family

"Does everyone have a family?" asked Tom as his mum tucked him into bed. "I suppose so", said his mum.

"Everyone in the whole world?" asked Tom. "Well," said Mum, "some people might not have a family."

"Why not?" asked Tom.

"Well, their family might have died or got lost in a war or a disaster."

Tom thought for a moment. "And would they be sad?"

"Yes", said Mum. "It must be very sad to lose your family, but don't worry, you won't lose us."

"Not ever?" said Tom.

"Well, perhaps when you are grown up", replied Mum.

"I know someone who hasn't got a family", said Tom suddenly.

"Oh dear", said Mum. "That's very sad. Who is it?"

"It's Teddy", replied Tom. "He hasn't got a family."

"Aren't we Teddy's family?" asked Mum.

"We are in a way," said Tom, "but we're not his real family. Tomorrow I'll give Teddy a family of his own."

"What a good idea", said Mum, smiling. "I have an old Teddy of mine who can be his grandma."

Tom smiled a tired smile. He was so happy because tomorrow Teddy would have a real family of his own.

[Affix school letterhead if required]

Dear Parent/Guardian,

Can you help?
In preparation for a lesson we are having it would be very helpful if you could read this letter from your child.

My family

At school we are going to talk about our family.

Please could you tell me:

- How many people are in our family?
- Who is the eldest person in our family?
- Who is the youngest person in our family?
- Can you tell me anything specially interesting about anyone in our family?

Thank you for helping me,

8 Sharing

Aims

- to help the children to become aware of all the things in our environment that we share with each other.
- to produce a sharing tree, that all the children helped to make.

Preparation

Draw a picture of a tree, with branches (but no leaves) on a large sheet of plain paper. Write the heading "This is our sharing tree. We all helped to make it."

Collect together counters or toys which can be used with the **Fair shares song** and make a suitable selection of number cards.

Before the lesson, send home photocopies of the **Can you help? copymaster** for discussion between the child and parent/guardian.

Make enough copies of the **Leaves for the sharing tree copymaster** so that all the children can have one each.

Make photocopies of the **Fair shares song**, as necessary.

Discussion

Points to bring out

- The importance of sharing, and how sharing involves cooperation, compassion and generosity to others.
- That the thing we share most with others is ourselves.

Strategies to try

Collect in the **Can you help? copymasters** and use the lists to prompt children during the discussion.

Do you share things at home?
What sort of things do we share with our families?
Do we share things at school?
Shall we make a little collection of things we share in the class? *(This could be put on display with a suitable label.)*
What shall we put in our collection? (*At this point the need to take turns could be emphasized.*)
Can any of you guess what is the nicest thing to share? (*after taking suggestions – OURSELVES!*)
When do we share ourselves with others? (*When we talk, when we play, when we take partners, when we help, when we listen.*)

Follow-up activity

Ask the children to look at the **Sharing tree** and ask:

What's missing? (*the leaves*)

Get each child to choose one leaf from the **Leaves for the sharing tree copymaster** to colour in, cut out and stick on the **Sharing tree**.

Song

Put the children into pairs and get each pair, in turns, to sing the **Fair shares song**. When they reach the last line of the song hold up a number card (even or odd). Hand out that number of counters or toys to the pair and ask the children to share them out fairly between them. In discussion the children must decide what to do if, after 'fair sharing', one item is left over. The game can be extended by grouping the children into threes or fours, etc.

Leaves for the sharing tree

Fair shares

(A singing game sung to the tune of "This Old Man".)

We can share

We can share

When we share we show we care

One for you and one for me

What do we do if we've got ________?

(Hold up a number card.)

[Affix school letterhead if required]

Dear Parent/Guardian,

Can you help?
In preparation for a lesson we are having it would be very helpful if you could read this letter from your child.

Sharing

At school we are going to talk about sharing. Could you make a list for me of some of the things we share at home (e.g. television, outings)?

At home we share:

____

____

____

____

____

____

Please will you remind me to put this list in my school bag and give it to my teacher?

Thank you for helping me,

My family and friends

TEAMWORK

9 Things we can do together

Aim

▶ to get the children to think about all the things that we do together, and so introduce the concept of teamwork.

Preparation

Before the lesson, send home photocopies of the **Can you help? copymaster** for discussion between the child and parent/guardian.

To assist the discussion, make some large word cards with the words "play", "shop" and "read" written on them. It would help if the cards were brightly decorated.

Make enough photocopies of the **Matching pairs copymaster**, so that all of the children can have a sheet each.

Make copies of the **Noah and his Ark copymaster**, as necessary.

Discussion

Points to bring out

- We can all do lots of things.
- Many of the things that we do, we do with others – sometimes with members of our family, sometimes with our friends.

Strategies to try

We are going to talk about things we can do with our family and friends. I've got some words to show you. (*Hold up word cards.*)

(*First word.*) This says play.
Who can we play with? What can we play together at school? What can we play together at home? Are the games we play with our friends the same games we play with our families?

(*Next word.*) This says shop.
Who can we shop with? Can you ever help with the shopping? How? When you are shopping do you see other families together? What sort of shopping do you like best?

(*Next word.*) This says read.
Who can we read with? Who has a bed-time story? Who likes listening to a story? Where do you hear the best stories?

Follow-up activity

Each child is given a **Matching pairs copymaster** and matches the pairs by cutting them out and sticking them on to a sheet of paper.

Game

Sit the children in a circle (the Ark) and chose one child to be Noah. The circle of children chant and clap the song from the **Noah and his Ark copymaster** while Noah skips around the outside of the circle. On the word "YET" Noah stops. The child that Noah stops behind goes into the circle and mimes an animal. Whoever guesses the animal then joins the mimer in the circle to make the pair of that animal. The game is repeated until the Ark is full.

Matching pairs

Cut out the figures and match the pairs.

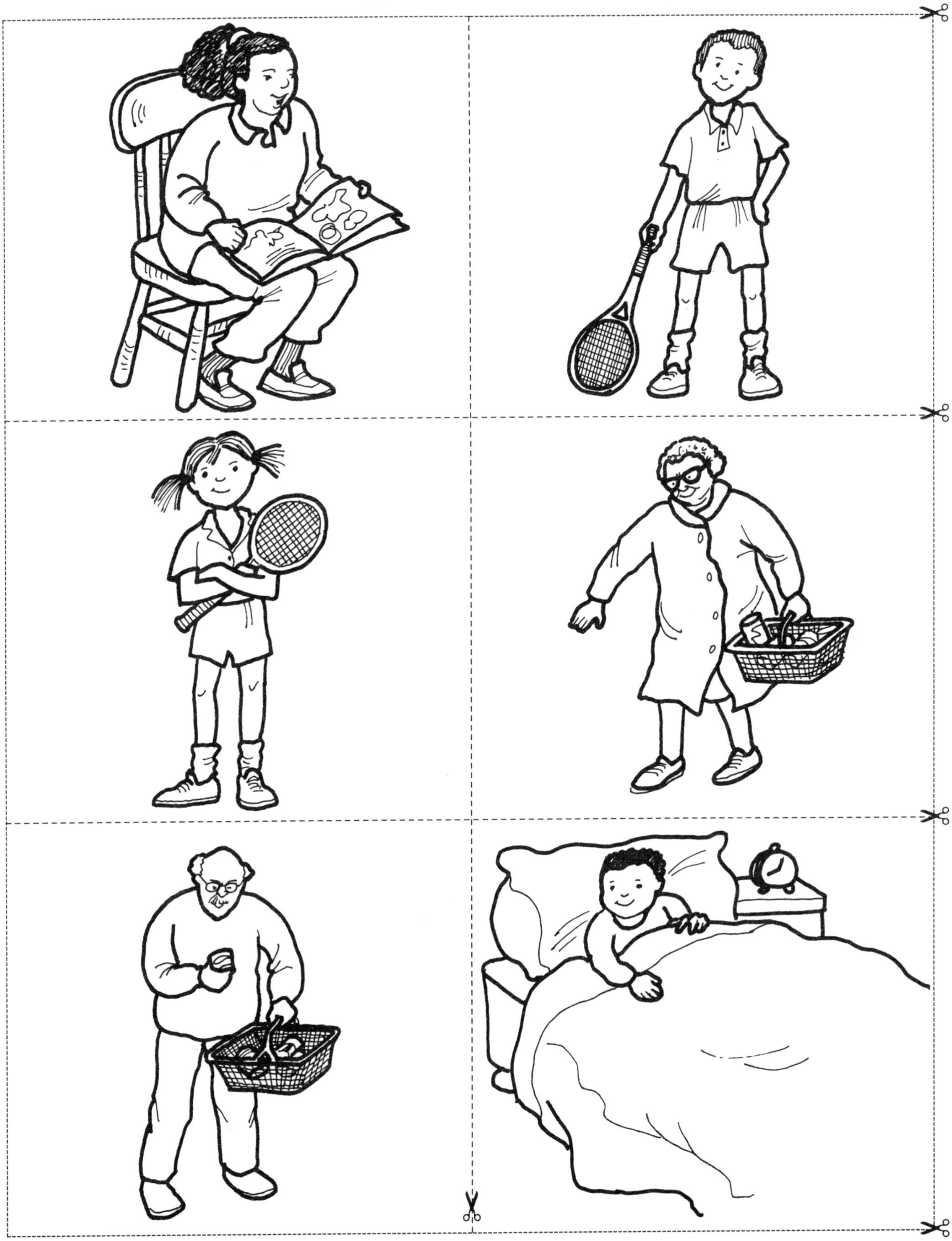

Noah and his Ark

(A singing game.)

It's raining
    It's raining
We're all getting wet
    Can we go?
Can we go?
    Into the ark YET!

[Affix school letterhead if required]

Dear Parent/Guardian,

Can you help?
In preparation for a lesson we are having it would be very helpful if you could read this letter from your child.

Things we can do together

At school we are going to talk about all the different things that we can do together as part of a lesson called "Things we can do together".

Please could you tell me:

- What things do all the family do together?
- What things do we do with friends?
- Are there any things that we can only do with the help of others?

Thank you for helping me,

My family and friends

CARING COMMUNITY

10
Who looks after me?

Aims

- to make children aware of how they are cared for at home and at school.
- to lead the children on to think about how they are part of, and can contribute to, a 'caring' community.

Preparation

Before the lesson, send home photocopies of the **Can you help? copymaster** for discussion between the child and parent/guardian.

To aid the discussion, collect a good selection of pictures of people who help children (e.g. crossing wardens, police officers, doctors, dentists, opticians, shop assistants, bus drivers, etc). It would also be good to have some pictures of people who need help (e.g. a very old person, a baby, someone with a pushchair and heavy shopping).

Make enough copies of the **Award for looking after... copymaster**, so that the children can all have one each, and write in each child's name.

Make copies of the **Who looks after me? song**, as necessary.

Discussion

Points to bring out

- We all need help at different times and in different ways.
- There are a great variety of people who help us.
- It is good to give and receive help.

Strategies to try

Let's look at some pictures of people who help to look after us.

Who is this person? (*Discuss the pictures of the helpers.*)
How can this person help us?
Have any of you had help today?
When do you think you have had help?
Who was it who looked after you?
Is it nice to have people to look after us?

Here are some people who might need to be looked after (*Show pictures*).
In what ways do you think they need help?
Can we ever look after someone? How?
Could we help someone today?

Follow-up activity

Each child selects someone who looks after them, decorates the rosette on the **Award for looking after... copymaster** and takes it home.

Song

After every verse stop singing and ask the children to answer the question posed in the **Who looks after me? song**. If necessary, be prepared to discuss, in depth, possible answers with the children.

The song also offers the opportunity to address special issues by adding third lines which deal with specific topics, for example: "When I'm lost and on my own"; "When I'm being bullied"; "When I cry and feel alone"; "When I need to say I'm sorry."

Award for looking after

Who looks after me?

(A song sung to the tune of "The Farmer's in his Den".)

Who looks after me?
Who looks after me?
When I'm feeling hungry
Who do I go and see?

[Children answer]

Who looks after me?
Who looks after me?
If I'm not feeling well
Who do I go and see?

[Children answer]

Who looks after me?
Who looks after me?
When my teeth need looking at
Who do I go and see?

[Children answer]

[Affix school letterhead if required]

Dear Parent/Guardian,

Can you help?
In preparation for a lesson we are having it would be very helpful if you could read this letter from your child.

Who looks after me?

At school we are going to talk about people who help us, as part of our lesson called "Who looks after me?"

Please could you tell me:

- Who looks after me at home?
- Can you tell me some of the things they do?
- Who looks after me at school?
- Can you tell me some of the things they do?
- How can I help people more?

Thank you for helping me,

11 Happy and sad

RESPECT FOR OTHERS

Aims

- ▶ to show that our actions often have an effect on how other people feel.
- ▶ to lead the children on to develop an understanding of the importance of respect for others, their property, and their feelings.

Preparation

Before the lesson, send home photocopies of the **Can you help? copymaster** for discussion between the child and parent/guardian.

Pre-read **The lost button story**. It would make this story come alive if you could build the story around some item the children could actually see and hold. If you can bring in a more suitable item to use when telling the story then you will need to adapt the story accordingly.

Make enough copies of the **Somewhere safe copymaster** so that all the children can have one each.

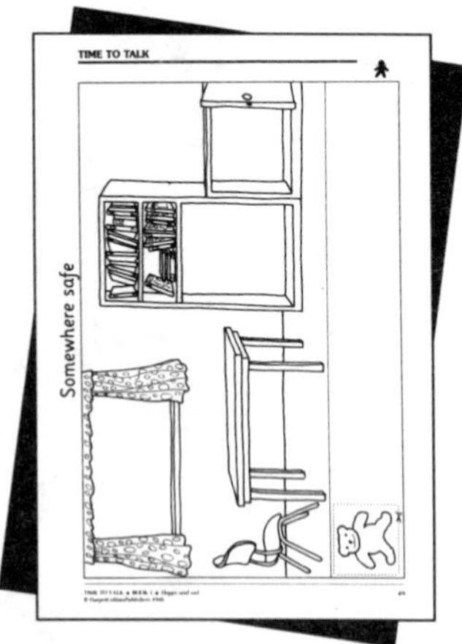

Make photocopies of **The lost button story**, as necessary.

Discussion

Points to bring out

- When we behave badly we feel bad about ourselves.
- Other people sometimes suffer as a result of our actions.
- We shouldn't do things to other people that we wouldn't want them to do to us.

Strategies to try

Read **The lost button story** to the children. Then continue:

Nigel did take his button to school and showed it to the teacher. The teacher told him to put it somewhere safe. Nigel put his button in a tray with his name on. After playtime the teacher asked Nigel to get his button and tell the class about it. But when he went to his tray the button was gone.

Ask the childre: What do you think had happened to it?

Nigel looked and looked, but someone had taken the button. Nigel was so sad that he began to cry. The teacher was sad that someone in her class had taken the button, and the children were sad because Nigel was crying. Soon even the girl who had taken the button began to feel upset. She had taken the button because she wanted it, but now she was sorry. She wanted to give the button back, but she didn't want anyone to know that she had taken it. Then the teacher said, "If you have the button and are frightened to give it back, please leave it somewhere where we can find it."

The story has a happy ending. The button was left beside the reading books. Nigel was so happy. The teacher was happy and the children were happy. But happiest of all was the girl who had taken the button, because the teacher and her class friends had helped her to give it back.

Ask the children: If you really wanted the button would you take it? How would you feel if something of yours was taken? What happy things were there in the story? What sad things were there in the story?

Follow-up activity

Hand out copies of the **Somewhere safe copymaster** and ask each child to cut out the teddy and glue it in a safe place in the picture.

Somewhere safe

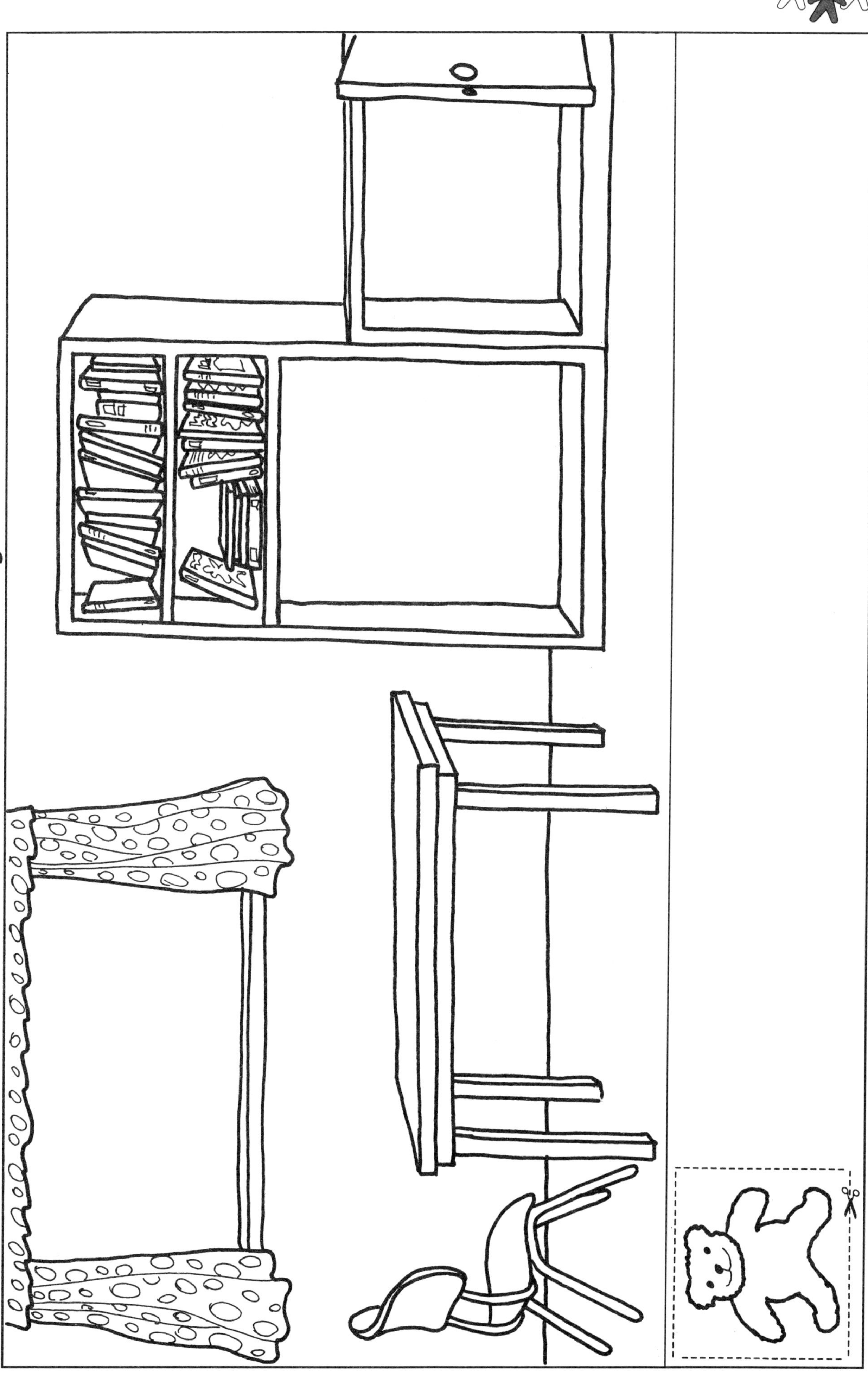

The lost button

When Nigel visited his grandma he was given a present. It was a button. You may think that a button is not a very good thing to give someone as a present, but this button was special. It was brass and had an anchor on it.

"This button belonged to your great-granddad", his grandma explained. "He was my dad. He was in the Navy. Of course that was long before you were born. When I was a little girl he would come home in his sailor's clothes and sit me on his knee and tell me about all the places he had been."

"Was he a captain?" asked Nigel.

"No", said Grandma. "He was a stoker. He shovelled the coal that made the steam engines go. That's the sort of engines ships had in those days."

"Was he in the war?" asked Nigel.

"Yes, love", replied Gran. "He was in the First World War. His ship was sunk at Jutland."

"Did he drown?" asked Nigel.

"Yes, dear", said Gran. "We were all very sad when we got the news. Lots of children lost their dads in that war."

Nigel and his gran talked about his great-granddad till it was time to go home.

"I'll take my button to school", said Nigel, "to show my friends."

"That's a good idea", said Gran. "And you can tell them all about your great-granddad."

On his way home Nigel kept tight hold of his button. He decided that it was the best present that he had ever had.

[Affix school letterhead if required]

Dear Parent/Guardian,

Can you help?
In preparation for a lesson we are having it would be very helpful if you could read this letter from your child.

Happy and sad

At school we are going to have a lesson called "Happy and sad".

Please could you tell me:

- Do I ever make you feel happy?
- How do I make you feel happy?
- Do I ever make you feel sad?
- How do I make you feel sad?
- How can I help people at home to be happy?

Thank you for helping me,

LEARNING COOPERATION

12

We like to play

Aim

▶ to teach, though play, the importance of working together.

Preparation

Before the lesson, send home photocopies of the **Games, games, games copymaster** and the **Can you help? copymaster**. Get the children to ask older or grown up friends to read the **Games, games, games copymaster** to them and to explain the games. It may also be helpful to play the games described on the copymaster before you begin the lesson, so that the children have some recent experience of co-operative games to draw on.

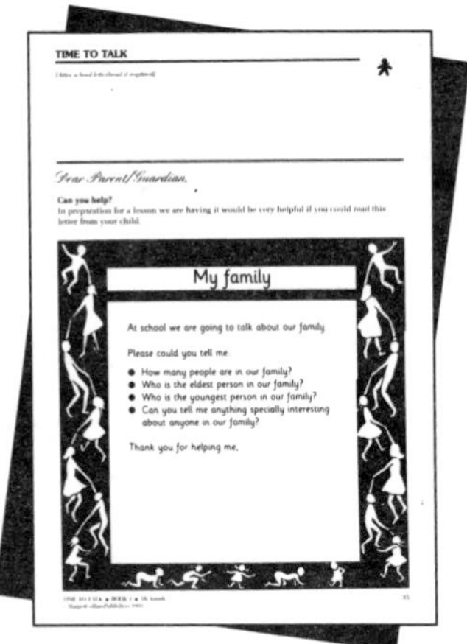

TIME TO TALK

Dear Parent/Guardian,

Can you help?

In preparation for a lesson we are having it would be very helpful if you could read this letter from your child.

My family

At school we are going to talk about our family

Please could you tell me:

- How many people are in our family?
- Who is the eldest person in our family?
- Who is the youngest person in our family?
- Can you tell me anything specially interesting about anyone in our family?

Thank you for helping me.

Make enough copies of the **Collecting flowers game** so that each pair of children can have one each.

Discussion

Points to bring out

- We like to play games with others.
- For the game to be a good game we need to co-operate with others, take turns and follow the rules.

Strategies to try

What do you like to do at playtime?

Who likes to play games? (*Encourage the children to talk about what they do and who they do it with.*)

Who plays games at home?

Who do you play with?

Where do you play?

Does anyone like to play on their own and not with others? (*Lead the discussion to show that it's fine to spend time on your own but it's also nice to play with others.*)

Who has a favourite game they would like to tell us about? (*Collect information about the games they play.*)

Follow-up activity

Put the children into pairs and give a copy of the **Collecting flowers game** to each pair. Give them a set of counters each (either 5 black or 5 white). The children can then play the game together. They must take it in turns to put one counter on each flower. When all the flowers are covered by a counter decide who is the winner. As the winner will always be the child who puts the first counter down, ask the children to think of a fairer way of determining who wins, e.g. the first child to put 3 counters down in a line (horizontal, vertical or diagonal).

Collecting flowers

Games, games, games

1. Who's got the bean bag?

One child stands at the front of a group of children with his/her back to the group. The child throws a bean bag over their head to the group behind. One child from the group retrieves the bean bag and hides it behind their back. When the bean bag is 'hidden' the children shout "Ready". The child at the front turns and tries to guess who's got the bean bag. If they are right, they have another turn. If they are wrong, the child who has the bean bag goes to the front and repeats the process. Make sure that the children in the group do not fight over possession of the bean bag, but take turns to retrieve and hide it.

2. What time is it, Mr Wolf?

One child (the wolf) stands at the front of a group of children with his/her back to them. The group stand a reasonable distance away. The children shout "What time is it, Mr Wolf?" The wolf answers with a time – one o'clock, two o'clock, three o'clock, etc. The group must move forward the number of steps called out as "o'clock". After three goes the children ask "What time is it, Mr Wolf?" to which the wolf replies "tea time" and turns and tries to catch one child. If a child is caught they are 'eaten' and out of the game. The wolf then has another go. If, however, by taking the right number of steps one of the children in the group can touch the wolf before tea time that child becomes the wolf.

3. This is the house that Jack built.

The children form a ring and hold hands. In the middle stands one child 'Jack' (or Jane). The children move round Jack chanting: "This is the house that Jack built, that Jack built, that Jack built. This is the house that Jack built, what do you want?" Jack then points at one child in the ring. If the child can name a household item e.g., a chair, tea-pot, etc then that child joins Jack in the middle. The process is repeated until the house is full (i.e. the circle of children is too small to go round the children collected in the middle). The end of the game is signalled by chaos as the children try to go round but can't!

[Affix school letterhead if required]

Dear Friend,

Can you help?
In preparation for a lesson we are having it would be very helpful if you could read this letter from one of our children.

We like to play

At school we are going to talk about games we play with our friends at school as part of a lesson called "We like to play".

Can you read the "Games, games, games" copymaster to me and explain how the games described on the copymaster are played?

- What games did you play with your friends when you were my age?
- Do you still play games with your friends, now that you are older?
- What games do you and your friends play now?
- What was your favourite game when you were my age?
- What is your favourite game now?

Thank you for helping me,

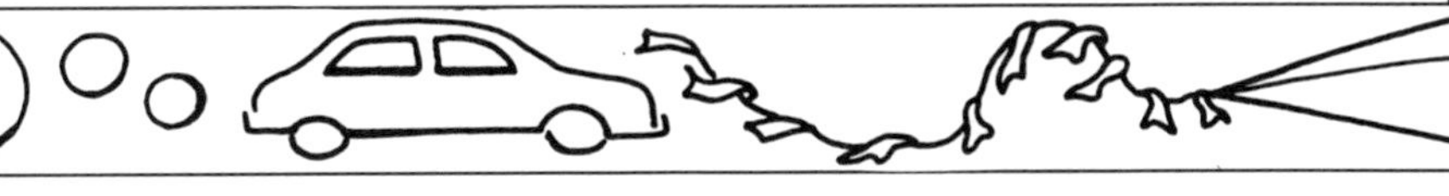

13 My house

UNDERSTANDING THE CREATED ENVIRONMENT

Aim

▶ to help children to develop an awareness of their own home environment.

Preparation

Before the lesson, send home photocopies of the **Can you help? copymaster** for discussion between the child and the parent/guardian.

Make enough A3 copies of the **My house copymaster** so that each group/table of children can have one each.

Make copies of the **The house that we built song**, as necessary.

On a large piece of A3 paper draw a simple outline of a house and make enough photocopies of it so that every group/table can have a copy. Keep a copy for yourself and clip it to a rigid backing so that it can be held up and drawn on.

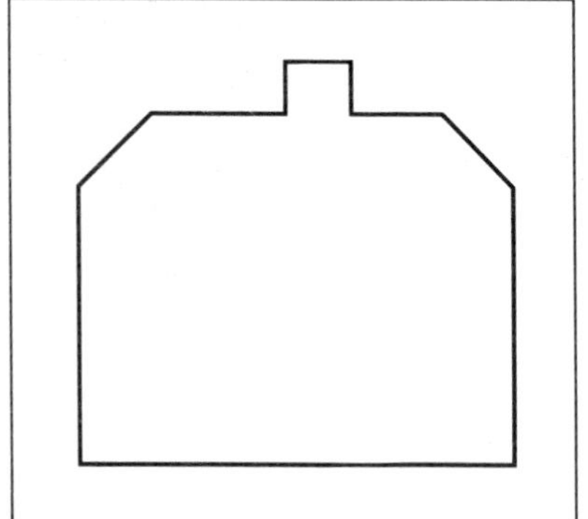

Collect varied selection of pictures of house types – bungalows, detached, semis, terraced, flats, caravans, etc – to show the children during the discussion.

Discussion

Points to bring out

- There are a various styles and types of homes, but they all have the same function – to keep us safe, warm and dry.

Strategies to try

Show the children the pictures you have collected and help them to identify the different types of houses that people live in.

Let's look at some houses.
Which one looks most like yours?
Do all our houses look the same?
Why do we think people live in houses?

Follow-up activity

Give each group/table a copy of the A3 outline house and an A3 copy of the **My house copymaster**. Ask the children to cut out pictures from the copymaster and glue them on to their house.

Song

The children can then sing the **The house that we built song** to help you to complete your outline house. As the children come to the last line of the song ask for suggestions of items that they could add to the house. Draw each new feature as it is suggested by the children.

Does anyone live in a house that looks like this?
Why do houses have doors and windows?
Why does the roof slope?
Is the house finished now? Is there anything missing?

Keep on going until the children run out of ideas.

My house

The house that we built

This is the house that we built.

This is the house that we built.

This is the __________ that went in the house that we built

[Affix school letterhead if required]

Dear Parent/Guardian,

Can you help?
In preparation for a lesson we are having it would be very helpful if you could read this letter from your child.

My house

At school we are going to talk about the different types of houses that people live, in as part of a lesson called "My house".

Please could you tell me:

- How many windows does our house have?
- How many doors does our house have?
- How do we keep our house warm when it is cold outside?
- Are all houses the same as ours?
- Can you tell me the some of the names of the types of houses that people might live in?

Thank you for helping me,

14
Shopping

ECONOMIC UNDERSTANDING

Aim

- ▶ to get children to share and compare common experiences.
- ▶ to attempt to establish why people shop.

Preparation

Find an older person (perhaps a parent) who can come into the classroom and talk about shopping. Ask them to go through the questions on the **Can you help? copymaster**. Make sure that the visitor is someone who can listen as well as talk to very young children. If the visitor has time to listen, get the children to recite the **I went to the shops poem**, as an introduction to the discussion.

Before the lesson send home photocopies of the **Can you help? copymaster** for discussion between the child and parent/guardian.

Make enough copies of the **What shop? copymaster** so that the children can have one each.

Make copies of the **I went to the shops poem**, as necessary.

TIME TO TALK

I went to the shops

I went to the shops to buy a penny sweet
I took it home to eat it, just for a treat.

I went to the shops to buy a currant bun
I took it home to eat it, just for fun.

I went to the shops to buy a piece of cheese
I took it home to eat it, just how I please.

I went to the shops to buy a loaf of bread
I took it home to eat it, before I went to bed

Discussion

Points to bring out

- There are different ways of shopping and different kinds of shops.
- Some shops specialize in selling particular goods (e.g. bakers, butchers, newsagents).

Strategies to try

The **Can you help? copymaster** will have thrown up many differences between the ways different people shop. For example many parents will buy all their goods from one big shop, while others may shop in specialist shops – buying their bread from a bakers, fish from a fishmongers, etc. The way people shop will depend on the area that they live in (is there a large supermarket locally?) and their own needs (smaller local shops may be easier to get to, or may supply specialist foods not available in supermarkets).

Ask the visitor to go through the questions on the **Can you help? copymaster** and to talk about why they shop the way they do.

The children are then invited to talk about what they know about going shopping.

Who goes shopping?
Who do you go with?
Where do you go?
What sort of shopping do you like best?
What sort of things do you buy?

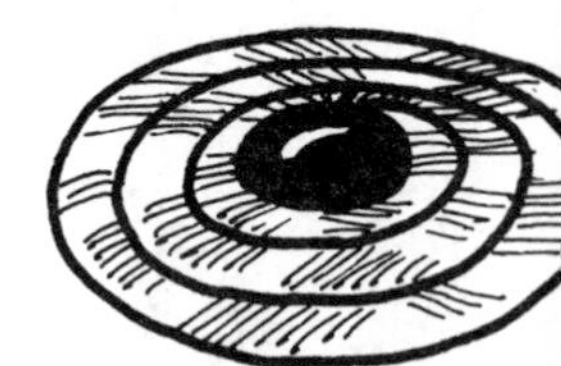

Follow-up activity

Give out the copies of the **What shop? copymaster** and ask the children to decide what sort of shop the window could belong to, and then to fill the window with pictures of appropriate items.

What shop?

THE LITTLE SHOP

I went to the shops

I went to the shops to buy a penny sweet
I took it home to eat it, just for a treat.

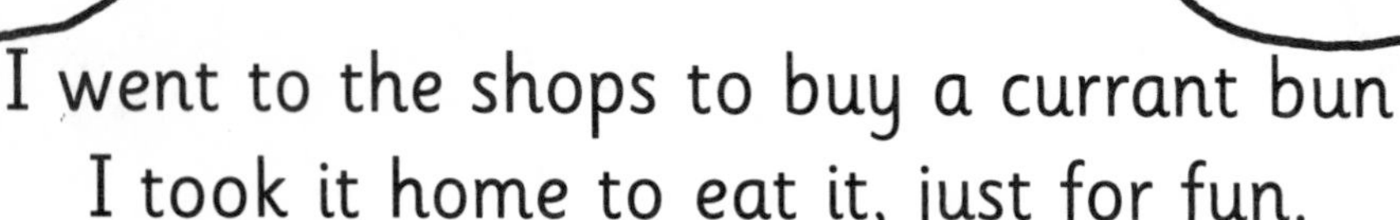

I went to the shops to buy a currant bun
I took it home to eat it, just for fun.

I went to the shops to buy a piece of cheese
I took it home to eat it, just how I please.

I went to the shops to buy a loaf of bread
I took it home to eat it, before I went to bed.

[Affix school letterhead if required]

Dear Parent/Guardian,

Can you help?
In preparation for a lesson we are having it would be very helpful if you could read this letter from your child.

Shopping

At school we are going to be talking about shopping.

Please can you tell me:

Where would you buy:

- Sweets?
- Medicine?
- Birthday cards?
- Bread?

Do you like shopping?
Can you tell me how you do your shopping?

Thank you for helping me,

15

If I was lost

PERSONAL SAFETY

Aim

▶ to present, in a non-threatening way, facts about how to cope with being lost.

Preparation

Invite an adult to tell a made-up story of when they were lost as an adult. The story must be realistic and, if possible, placed locally. A suggestion is that the adult was taken by a friend to a shop or market to look around, then left alone. They thought that they could make their own way to meet the friend but got lost. The story should have a happy, and realistic, ending provided by the adult following a correct procedure (asking for help from a policeman/someone well known to them, etc.)
In choosing the adult to work with, a non-uniform police officer may be a good choice if one is available and willing. Certainly check with an appropriate authority for advice and suggestions on the sensible procedures that a small child should follow if they become lost.

Before the lesson, send home photocopies of the **Can you help? copymaster** for discussion between the child and the parent/guardian.

Make enough copies of the **Hide and seek copymaster**, so that the children can all have one each.

Make copies of the **Teddy's lost song**, as appropriate.

Discussion

Points to bring out

- You don't only get lost when you are on your own – you can easily get lost in a crowd – so stick close to the person you are with.
- You don't have to be in a strange place to get lost – even familiar places can sometimes be confusing.

Strategies to try

The visiting adult is introduced. They tell a story (which you have already approved) about being lost. Encourage the children to ask questions:

How did you know you were lost?
How did you feel?
How did you decide who to ask for help?

It is vital to ensure that any suggestions for action by a lost child are both appropriate and clear.

Follow-up activity

Getting lost and being alone isn't always frightening. You can play at getting lost. What do we call the game when you hide and your friends try and find you? (Hand out copies of the **Hide and seek copymasters**.)

During the activity emphasize that hide and seek is a fun game, but that it is not fun to pretend to be lost or to play hide and seek in dangerous or unfamiliar places.

Song

Choose a pupil. The rest of the class sing the **Teddy's lost song**, with their eyes closed, while Teddy is hidden somewhere in the classroom. At the end of the song the pupil chosen must find Teddy before a given count (chanted and clapped by the class) is done. All the children can then have a go at colouring in the **Teddy's lost song** and finding Teddy in the picture.

Hide and seek

Help Jenny to find her friends.

Teddy's lost

(A singing game sung to the tune of "Ba-ba Black Sheep".)

Teddy's lost
Teddy's lost
We must find him at all cost
Is he in the classroom?
Can we see?
Who will bring my teddy to me?
Teddy's lost
Teddy's lost
We must find him at all cost

[Affix school letterhead if required]

Dear Parent/Guardian,

Can you help?
In preparation for a lesson we are having it would be very helpful if you could read this letter from your child.

If I was lost

At school we are talking about being lost. Could you look at this picture with me and tell me: Is anyone in this picture lost? What should they do? Who should they ask for help?

Where I live

16
Where I live

PERSONAL ENVIRONMENT

Aim

▶ to help children to appreciate their personal environment.

Preparation

Before the lesson, send home photocopies of the **Can you help? copymaster** for discussion between the child and the parent/guardian.

Make enough copies of the **Where I live copymaster**, so that the children can all have one each.

Make copies of the **My window poem**, as necessary.

Discussion

Points to bring out

- There are many different places that we call 'home'.

Strategies to try

Collect in all the replies from the **Can you help? copymaster**. (Put names on all the responses.) Those who haven't brought back a reply should try to remember something that they have seen from their window so that it can be written on their sheets.

Once this is done say this verse:

Guess what I can see?
Guess what I can see?
When I look out my window
Guess what I can see?

Then call out one of the responses from the **Can you help? copymaster**. The children have to guess whose response it is. They are allowed 3 guesses. If no one has guessed, the person is asked to stand up. Each person whose view is chosen is encouraged to talk a little bit about the view from their window.

The discussion can be brought to a conclusion by highlighting the similarities and differences about the places the children live.

Follow-up activity

Give each child a copy of the **Where I live copymaster** and ask them to draw and colour in a view from their bedroom window. The **Can you help? copymaster** can be refered back to if any child has problems deciding what to draw.

Where I live

Draw and colour in the view from your bedroom window

My window

If you sit at my window
And look outside with me,
I think you will be quite surprised
To see what you can see.

When I look out my window
And look up to the sky,
I often see a space ship
As it goes flying by.

When I look out my window
And I keep very still,
The elephants upon the lawn
Give me a special thrill.

When I look out my window
After I have had my tea,
I like to see the sailing ships
That pass upon the sea.

When I look out my window
In the darkness of the night,
I do not let the lions know
That they give me a fright.

When I look out my window
Before I go to bed,
A kangaroo waves up at me,
I think his name is Fred.

If you sit at my window
And look outside with me,
I think you will be quite surprised
To see what you can see.

[Affix school letterhead if required]

Dear Parent/Guardian,

Can you help?
In preparation for a lesson we are having it would be very helpful if you could read this letter from your child.

Where I live

In school we are going to be talking about places where we live. Please will you sit with me and talk about all of the things that we can see from my bedroom window. Then choose just one thing and write about it and send our ideas to school.

From my window I can see ____________________

____

____

____

____

____

Please will you remind me to put this list in my school bag and give it to my teacher?

Thank you for helping me,

17 What I do after school

DEVELOPING LEARNING SKILLS

Aim

- to encourage children to develop the skills of asking, listening and reporting.

Preparation

Before the lesson, send home photocopies of the **Can you help? copymaster** for discussion between the child and the parent/guardian.

You will need some large envelopes (they may be ones already used) and slips of paper for the children to put into the envelopes.

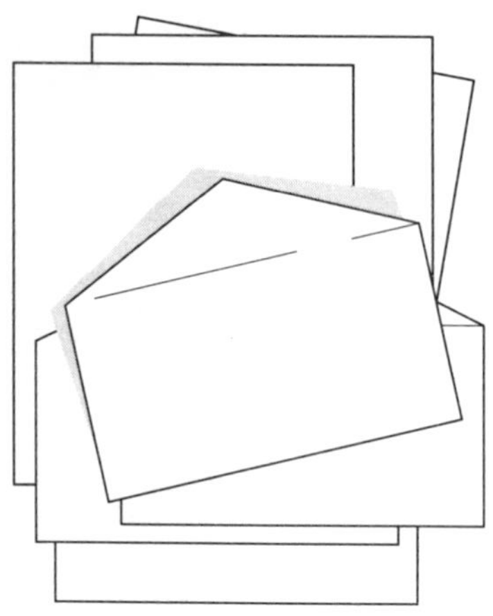

Make enough copies of the **What I do after school copymaster** so that the children can all have one each.

Make copies of the **After school song**, as necessary.

Discussion

Points to bring out

- We all do lots of things – some things will be different, some will be the same, like eating or going to bed.

Strategies to try

Make a list of all the things that the children do after school (e.g. eating, watching TV, playing with friends, washing, going to bed). Write each item on the front of an envelope and pin the envelopes up on the wall. Some activities, e.g. 'play with friends' or 'play with parents' can be put in the same category (in this case 'play').

Each child is given a partner in the class. (In the event of an odd number one child can be paired with an available adult.) Each child then asks their partner the question: What do you like doing *best* after school? Everyone listens while they do this. This needs to be carefully structured. The children first need to be comfortably partnered. As young children cannot readily hold information for a long time and then recall it, ask each pair to work in turn out loud, lending assistance as required. This develops the skills of asking and listening.

As children give answers they take it in turns to put a slip of paper in the appropriate envelope. The children can then talk about which activity they think is the most popular. This tests recall.

Slips can then be taken out of the envelopes and counted to see which activity is the most popular.

Follow-up activity

Each child is given or allowed to choose one activity that they like to do after school to record as a picture in the **What I do after school copymaster**. These pictures can then be bound together to make a class book.

Song

Use the after school activities suggested by the children to sing the **After school song**. Try to get the children to arrange the activities in a logical order, starting with 'going home' and ending with 'go to bed'.

Suggestions for appropriate verse endings could include: "go on home", " watch TV", "eat our tea", "play with our friends", "talk and talk", "go to bed".

Starting at the beginning how many verses can we remember?

What I do after school

After school

(A song sung to the tune of "Here We Go Round The Mulberry Bush".)

After school we __________ (x 3)
After school we __________ (x 1)
And this is how we do it

After school we __________ (x 3)
After school we __________ (x 1)
And this is how we do it

After school we __________ (x 3)
After school we __________ (x 1)
And this is how we do it

After school we __________ (x 3)
After school we __________ (x 1)
And this is how we do it

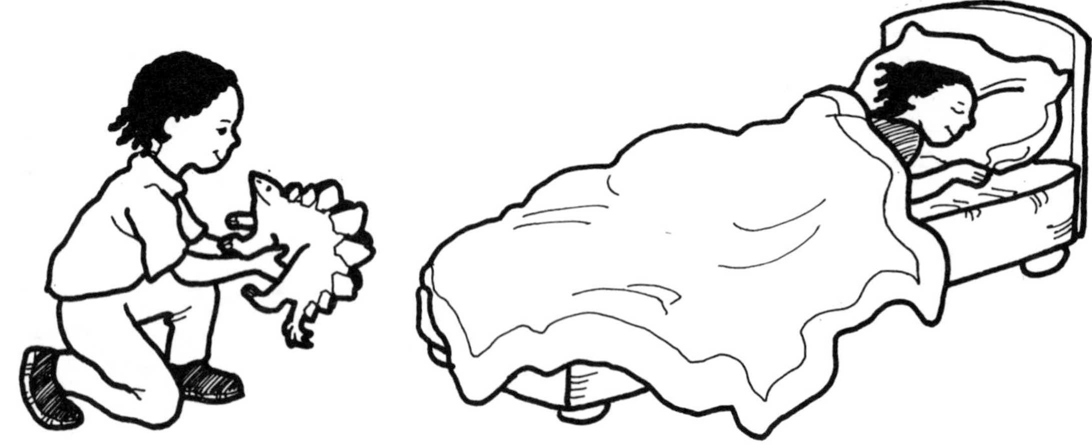

Can you think of actions to go with this song?

[Affix school letterhead if required]

Dear Parent/Guardian,

Can you help?
In preparation for a lesson we are having it would be very helpful if you could read this letter from your child.

What I do after school

We are going to have a lesson about things that we do after school. Please can you help me to think about all the things that I do when I get home?

Do I:

- Have something to eat?
- Watch TV?
- Play with my friends or brothers/sisters?
- Talk about what I did in school?

What else do I do?

Thank you for helping me,

Where I live

18

Saying no

ASSERTIVENESS

Aims

- to teach children about the dangers of approaching strangers.
- to help children develop the confidence to say 'no' in circumstances where a peer or an adult are trying to encourage them to do things which they know to be wrong.

Preparation

Before the lesson hand out photocopies of the **Can you help? copymaster** for discussion between the child and parent/guardian.

TIME TO TALK

Dear Parent/Guardian,

Can you help?
In preparation for a lesson we are having it would be very helpful if you could read this letter from your child.

Saying no

At school we are going to talk about times we should say 'no'

Please could you tell me

- About the times when you have to say 'no' (e.g. when you don't want to do something)
- How you feel when you have to say 'no'? (Good when you have to say no because you know it's not right, or bad when you have to disappoint or upset someone.)
- Times when you want me to say 'no' (e.g. saying no to strangers, or to silly friends)

Thank you for helping me.

Make enough copies of the **If you are called to a car copymaster** so that all the children can have one each.

Draw a line down the middle of a plain piece of A4 paper. In one half write yes, in the other half write no. Make enough copies so that all the children can have one each. Get the children to cut the sheet into two down the middle line and colour in the yes and no.

Discussion

Points to bring out

- Sometimes we have to think before saying 'yes' or 'no' and sometimes we all know the right answer straight away.

Strategies to try

Ask the children questions which concern their safety, and to which they can indicate a simple 'yes' or 'no' answer by holding up the yes or no cards that you have prepared. (The questions should be arranged so that sometimes the answer is yes and sometimes the answer is no.) The use of cards, rather than spoken answers or raised hands, should allow the children to respond unselfconsciously, without the fear of ridicule from classmates. If it is clear from the responses given that there is some uncertainty about what the correct answer is, the cards will also enable you to question responses and follow-up with further information without singling out any one child.

Should we always be careful crossing the road?
Should we play games on a busy road?
Should we ever go with someone we don't know?
Should we run off on our own?
Should we keep our class tidy?
Should we wear hats when it's wet?
Should we be kind to each other?

Follow-up activity

The **If you are called to a car copymaster** can be coloured in by the children as an introduction to further discussion – focusing on the dangers of talking to and going with strangers.

If you are called to a car

POLICE

Yes

No

[Affix school letterhead if required]

Dear Parent/Guardian,

Can you help?
In preparation for a lesson we are having it would be very helpful if you could read this letter from your child.

Saying no

At school we are going to talk about times we should say 'no'.

Please could you tell me:

- About the times when you have to say 'no' (e.g. when you don't want to do something).
- How you feel when you have to say 'no'? (Good when you have to say no because you know it's not right, or bad when you have to disappoint or upset someone.)
- Times when you want me to say 'no' (e.g. saying no to strangers, or to silly friends).

Thank you for helping me,

[Affix school letterhead if required]

Just to say a big

THANK YOU

for all the help you have given.

From

FURTHER RESOURCES

Answers – A cross-curricular programme for primary schools
The *Time to Talk* series covers PSHE up to age 7. *Answers*, also published by Collins Educational, covers PSHE for ages 7-11. The series comes in two packs – *Answers Pack 1*, ISBN 000 312006 6, (for ages 7-9) and *Answers Pack 2*, ISBN 000312007 4, (for ages 9-11). Each pack contains a 160-page, photocopiable teachers' book and twenty-four full colour A3 posters.

Collins Educational also publishes a wide range of resources which can be used to support the topics covered in the *Time to Talk* series.

Stories, poems and plays are a particularly effective way of teaching PSHE at this age range. Relevant Collins' titles include:

From the _Book Bus_ reading scheme packs –
My Turn, Your Turn; *Henrietta Gets a Blaster* (both dealing with the topic of consideration); *The Enormous Turnip* (team work); *Male and Female* (sex education); *Young and Old* (understanding ageing); *The Boy Who Cried Wolf* (honesty); *Gone for Good* (conservation).

From the Collins _Cascades_ series & _Young Lion Storybooks_ –
Cynthia Voigt, *A Solitary Blue*, ISBN 000 6726836 (loneliness and family break-up); Judith Kerr, *When Hitler Stole Pink Rabbit*, ISBN 000 6708013 (coping with change); Noel Streatfeild, *The Painted Garden*, ISBN 000 673765X (moving house); Rachel Anderson, *Paper Faces*, ISBN 000 674952X (family relationships); Ann Jungman, *Lucy Keeps the Wolf from the Door*, ISBN 000 6730507 (vegetarianism); Marlene Fanta Shyer, *Welcome Home Jellybean*, ISBN 000 3300188 (dealing with a handicapped child in the family); Gene Kemp, *Just Ferret*, ISBN 000 3300846 (bullying); Berlie Doherty, *Tough Luck*, ISBN 000 3300579 (starting a new school).

From the R.E.A.L. series
The *R.E.A.L* (Religion, Education and Life) *Infant Assembly Book*, ISBN 000 312004 X, includes work which can be linked directly to topics covered in *Time to Talk*. The R.E.A.L storybook *A Tapestry of Tales*, ISBN 000 312000 7, contains numerous moral stories from the six main religions.

If you would like to receive inspection copies of any of these titles, please write to:

Collins Educational, HarperCollins_Publishers_, FREEPOST GW 5078, Bishopbriggs, Glasgow G64 1BR.
Tel: 0141 306 3484. Fax: 0141 306 3750.